Thank you to PBS for playing films like Lilien's
Pale Male; the dedicated bird-watchers for keeping
the hawks safe; NYC Audubon; and my editor, Alex,
for immense help in researching this project.

SIMON & SCHUSTER BOOKS FOR YOUNG READERS
An imprint of Simon & Schuster Children's Publishing Division
1230 Avenue of the Americas, New York, New York 10020
Copyright © 2007 by Meghan McCarthy
All rights reserved, including the right of reproduction in
whole or in part in any form.
SIMON & SCHUSTER BOOKS FOR YOUNG READERS is a
trademark of Simon & Schuster, Inc.
Book design by Lucy Ruth Cummins
The text for this book is set in Graham.
The illustrations for this book are rendered in acrylic paint.
Manufactured in China
2 4 6 8 10 9 7 5 3 1
CIP data for this book is available from the Library of Congress.
ISBN-13: 978-1-4169-3359-5
ISBN-10: 1-4169-3359-X

first
edition

New York City Audubon

Two percent of the publisher's net proceeds from the sale of this book
through regular U.S. trade channels shall be donated to:

New York City Audubon
71 West 23rd Street, Room 1523
New York, NY 10010
www.nycaudubon.org

Net proceeds are the gross amounts received by the publisher less shipping,
mailing, and insurance costs or charges and taxes.

New York City Audubon is a grassroots community that works for the protection
of wild birds and habitat in the five boroughs, improving the quality
of life for all New Yorkers.

CITY HAWK

THE STORY OF PALE MALE

Written and illustrated by Meghan McCarthy

A Paula Wiseman Book
Simon & Schuster Books for Young Readers
New York   London   Toronto   Sydney

New York City is bustling with cars, buses, and people hurrying to important places. There are lots of tall buildings, lots of streets, and lots of pollution.

That's why so many people flock to the city's largest park for a needed escape. While in Central Park, New Yorkers can take a nap in the grass, play catch on one of the sprawling lawns, or get a glimpse of a squirrel scurrying up a tree.

What they never expect is to see real wildlife—
animals that usually make their homes in forests
or on mountaintops or by rivers.

Passersby couldn't believe their eyes when a red-tailed hawk was spotted flying over Fifth Avenue. Bird-watchers took an interest in the hawk. They named him Pale Male because of his light feathers. Day after day, month after month, Pale Male could be seen soaring high above Central Park.

After Pale Male was sighted near a pond in Central Park,

flying over the
Metropolitan Museum of Art,

and by a
hot-dog stand,
it was clear that he
was there to stay.

Every year the ritual began. . . .

One year Pale Male found a bird named Lola.
She was a hawk too. Her feathers were darker
than his, and she was bigger in size. Pale Male
dove and swooped and fluttered around Lola.

Together the two birds gathered twigs and branches
and piled them atop an apartment building overlooking
Central Park. Large spikes meant to ward off pigeons
made it easy for Pale Male and Lola to build a nest.
But what they didn't know was . . .

. . . they were being watched.

Across Fifth Avenue, into Central Park, and past a small body of water called the Boat Pond, a group of people watched the hawks intently. There were young people and old people, men and women. The most dedicated of these bird-watchers called themselves "the Regulars."

The Regulars carried big cameras and big telescopes. They watched the action excitedly like die-hard fans viewing their favorite sporting event. The question on everyone's mind was: Did Lola lay eggs?

Yes! But when would they hatch?

The Regulars arrived at the park before the sun came up
and didn't leave until the sun went down.

They waited in the rain. They waited in the dark.

They waited and waited and waited.

Finally the two babies were born! They chirped excitedly for food. Pale Male was a good dad and worked tirelessly to bring plenty of food back for them. The Regulars named one baby Handsome and the other Gretel.

When the babies grew enough feathers and became strong, it was time for them to fly. Most hawks usually practice flying by hopping from tree to tree . . . but there were no trees! The babies would have to leap off the tall building and fly across Fifth Avenue.

The fall down would be far.

They hopped . . .
and hopped . . .
and hopped some more . . .
but neither flew.

At last, one morning before the sun peeked above the trees, one baby took the first flight, disappearing into the dark blue sky.

The daylight brought new excitement. Soon both babies were exploring the park. The Regulars watched it all. Their early mornings and late nights in the park were worth every minute.

If you go to Central Park and you watch . . . and wait . . .
you may see a pale-feathered hawk. . . .

And come spring, chances are, there will be a nest.

Inside the nest there may be several eggs with babies, ready to greet the world.

Learn More About Central Park

In 1850, New York City was busy, noisy, and dirty. The only outdoor places that were open and quiet were cemeteries. Some people, however, didn't find the cemeteries too cheerful and wished for an alternative. For health reasons, too, an open space was needed. One man suggested building a park to become the "lungs of the city." It would be a place to sit, relax, and breathe.

In 1857 the city commissioners sponsored a competition to design what would become Manhattan's largest park, right in the middle of the city and equidistant from the east and west sides. The city commissioners chose a design created by two architects named Calvert Vaux and Frederick Law Olmsted.

But what a challenge making the park would be! The land was swampy, rocky, and downright unpleasant. Five hundred thousand cubic feet of topsoil was carted in. Four million trees, plants, and bushes were planted. Thirty-six bridges were built. Four bodies of water were created. It took many years and thousands of workers.

In the early years the park was pristine. There were model boat races at the Boat Pond; a carousel powered by real horses; a flock of pedigree sheep grazing in the area now known as Sheep Meadow; and for the first few years, real, brightly colored peacocks wandering around the park for all to enjoy. Vaux

Calvert Vaux

Frederick
Law Olmsted

and Olmsted's vision was to create a place for both the rich and poor to convene together, and the park did just that.

As time went by, however, things changed. The trees grew taller and the grass thicker. Some parts of the park were choked by vines and dead shrubbery. Even the sunlight had a hard time penetrating the overgrowth. Vaux and Olmsted's goal had been to create a park that looked natural, but what they hadn't intended on was grass that never got watered and brush that was left to grow too wild. By the 1970s, spray paint cropped up on the buildings and Central Park became synonymous with danger. Crime had risen, tourism was down, and some New Yorkers were afraid to venture into the park.

The park needed help. In 1980 the Central Park Conservancy, mostly privately funded out of the pockets of New York citizens, began extensive restoration. New drainage systems were put in, grass was dug up and reseeded, and spray paint was removed. Thanks to that dedicated group, the park is now in better shape than it's ever been. The lawns are always green, the streams are always running, and the trees are healthy and tall. Animals and birds such as Pale Male can now thrive, and both visitors and city dwellers can relax and enjoy the park, exactly as Vaux and Olmsted intended.

Visit www.palemalebook.com for more information about Central Park and Pale Male.

Bibliography

Central Park Conservancy. "150+ Years of Park History." Available at http://www.centralparknyc.org/centralparkhistory/cp-history-150 yrs. Accessed December 20, 2006.

Berenson, Richard J., and Raymond Carroll. *Barnes and Noble Complete Illustrated Map and Guidebook to Central Park*. New York: Silver Lining Books, 1999.

Berman, John S. *Portraits of America: Central Park*. New York: Barnes and Noble Books, 2003.

Blackmar, Elizabeth, and Roy Rosenzweig. "Central Park History." Central Park.com. October 19, 2006. Available at http://www.centralpark.com/pages/history.html. Accessed December 20, 2006.

Bullet, Mark, and Heidi Singer. "Hawk Fans Sink Talons in Co-op: Nature-Lovers Turning Up Heat in Avian 'Eviction' Flap." *New York Post*, December 11, 2004, p. 3.

DiGiacomo, Frank. "Ruffled Feathers on Fifth Avenue." *Vanity Fair*, July 2005, p. 106.

Haberman, Clyde. "So Much Squawking Is Heard, and Over Such a Cause." *New York Times*, December 14, 2004, B1.

Harvey, Adam. "The Lovebirds That Have All the New Yorkers Talking." *Sunday Telegraph*, April 30, 2006, p. 36.

Karim, Lincoln. http://www.palemale.com. Accessed throughout 2006.

Kinetz, Erika. "Neighborhood Report: New York Up Close; Not Just an Adored Bird, but a Hawk About Town." *New York Times*, April 28, 2006, section 14, p. 4.

Kinkead, Eugene. *Central Park 1857–1995: The Birth, Decline, and Renewal of a National Treasure*. New York: W. W. Norton & Co., 1990.

Knowler, Don. "Height of Passion." *Hobart Mercury* (Australia), July 1, 2006, B12.

Lee, Jennifer. "Pale Male and Lola Make an Inspection Tour." *New York Times*, December 29, 2004, B2.

Lee, Jennifer, and Thomas J. Lueck. "No Fighting the Co-op Board, Even with Talons." *New York Times*, December 11, 2004, A1.

Lilien, Frederic. *Pale Male*. Silver Spring, MD: Devillier Donegan Enterprises, 2002. Videorecording.

Lueck, Thomas J. "Four Hawks, Two Nests, One Empty." *New York Times*, April 21, 2006, B5.

———. "In Furor Over Displaced Hawks, Effort Is Made to Save the Nest." *New York Times*, December 14, 2004, B1.

———. "New Aerie Is Readied for Fifth Avenue Hawks." *New York Times*, December 22, 2004, B3.

———. "New York Celebrities Evicted on Fifth Ave., Feathers and All." *New York Times*, December 8, 2004, B1.

Miller, Sara Cedar. *Central Park: An American Masterpiece*. New York: Harry N. Abrams, Inc., 2003.

Petrak, Chris. "The Saga of Pale Male and Lola, Two Hawks in the Big Apple." *Brattleboro Reformer* (Vermont), March 25, 2005, Columnists Page.

Pinkerton, James P. "Fifth Avenue Calls of the Wild; Pale Male's Tale Inspires Those of Restless Spirit." *Newsday*, December 28, 2004, A33.

Putnam, Karen. *New York's 50+ Best Places to Enjoy Central Park*. New York: Universe Publishing, 2004.

Pyle, Richard. "Hawks' Fifth Avenue Nest Framework Is Reinstalled." *Associated Press*, December 23, 2004, State and Regional Wire.

———. "Manhattan's Famous Hawk Flies the Coop, Make That Co-op, for New West Wise Home." *Canadian Press*, June 6, 2006, Foreign General News Wire.

———. "New Yorker Presides from on High, as City Looks Up in Awe." *Associated Press*, June 5, 2004, State and Local Wire.

Segal, Dave. "Joy and Raptor on Fifth Avenue; Manhattan Co-op Reverses Decision to Evict Hawks." *Washington Post*, December 17, 2004, C1.

Seitz, Sharon. *Big Apple Safari for Families: The Urban Park Rangers' Guide to Nature in New York City*. Woodstock, VT: The Countryman Press, 2005.

Tierney, John. "The Big City: Newest Things to Watch: Hawk TV?" *New York Times*, May 17, 1999, B1.

Winn, Marie. *Red-Tails in Love*. New York: Vintage Departures, 2005.

Xiaoqing, Rong. "Watching Like Hawks." *South China Morning Post*, April 22, 2006, p. 17.

The magic of the Pale Male story is that it unites the very young and the very old, the very rich and the very homeless, in the relentless pursuit to soak up all that the Pale Male saga has to offer. Whether it's a balmy 65 degrees or a frigid, wind-whipping 20 degrees, if the hawk is there, the hawk watchers are too. To some, the idea of watching a bird groom its feathers for hours and fly back and forth from building to tree over and over again just to pick the right twig to bring to his nest, for weeks at a time—when one lives in a city full of celebrities, Broadway shows, and constant action—might seem perplexing; but once you peer into the telescope and see the dashing bird, chances are, you won't be able to look away. Perhaps you might even become a hawkaholic.

Each year thousands of hawks fly over New York City. Central Park is a major stop on the Atlantic Flyway, a key migration route for birds. Spotting a red-tailed hawk from afar in New York isn't an unusual occurrence. What *is* unusual is that a red-tailed bird of prey would choose to make New York City its home. In fact, Pale Male was documented as the first. After he settled in the city in 1991, bird experts were perplexed. "Maybe the male had a screw loose somewhere," commented Dr. Dean Amadon, curator of birds at the American Museum of Natural History.

But did he? Pale Male didn't just pick the business capital of the world; he happened to choose prime real estate. The co-op building was home to the likes of Mary Tyler Moore and other wealthy dwellers. Each apartment in the building is worth millions. Dr. Alexander Fisher, an avid bird watcher and next-door neighbor, noted in Frederic Lilien's documentary *Pale Male*, "They have been good neighbors. They are smart enough to pick out the most

beautiful apartment overlooking Central Park and getting away without paying for it, capiche?"

While the nest's position on the twelfth-floor cornice of 927 Fifth Avenue posed many risks for fledgling birds' first flights, it also had many advantages. Metal spikes intended to ward off pigeons and their unsightly droppings were beneficial to the red-tails by firmly holding the twigs in place and making their nest secure. The cornice also protected the baby birds against rain and winds. Although the building had the most picturesque views of the park, it had something else that only a hawk could find desirable—easy access to free dinner, and lots of it. Central Park's animal dwellers were not accustomed to dealing with a bird with sharp talons who swoops down in a surprise attack from a building across the street.

After several years of unsuccessful nesting attempts and several mates, Pale Male finally had a family in the spring of 1995. In addition, he also had a large extended family; a loyal following of hawk watchers could always be found across the street at the Boat Pond. It seemed that the longer the birds resided at 927 Fifth Avenue, the more high-powered and expensive equipment the hawk watchers came equipped with. Lincoln Karim, owner of PaleMale.com, often brought a telescope to the park, the kind used by astronomers to magnify tiny stars in the solar system. He connected his bird-viewing device to a 32-inch monitor, which allowed the crowd to watch in close detail. His "rig," as he called it, described by one reporter as a "unit resembling the Hubble Space Telescope," was a motorized go-cart that was computer-programmed to focus on Pale Male's favorite spots.

Waiting for the fledglings to make the first leap was always especially tense for hawk watchers. Crowds would gather. Bets

were placed. Nervous "parents" paced. There was a champagne toast to Pale Male on Father's Day and cookies decorated with black-and-white hawks to celebrate. The hawk fever was contagious.

Not everyone, however, was thrilled. Many of the building's dwellers wished the bird would go away. Who could blame them? Their expensive terraces were being watched night and day, and messy remains of hawk dinners often fell on their doorsteps. By 2004 the nest had become eight feet wide and weighed as much as four hundred pounds. "That ain't a regular nest," stated the building engineer who was hired to inspect the building. In the late afternoon of December 7, 2004, several men hired by the co-op to remove the nest began to dismantle it, one twig at a time, until not even the pigeon spikes remained. The hawk watchers' world crumbled.

It didn't take long for outrage to be expressed. Protestors gathered on Fifth Avenue with signs that read HONK 4 HAWKS and other messages of support. Two protestors even showed up wearing giant bird costumes. Mary Tyler Moore, co-op dweller and hawk supporter, said, "This was something we like to talk about: a kinder, gentler world, and now it's gone." While the commotion was going on below, Pale Male and his mate circled the building. Back and forth they flew from the building to the park, carrying small twigs and placing them where their nest had been, but without the pigeon spikes in place, the sticks just blew away.

What started as a candlelight vigil, which was contained to a small group of loyal Pale Male fans, soon grew into a spectacle that included protestors of all sorts. One co-op resident said, "Before there were just, I think, bird lovers. . . . And these are a peaceful group. . . . Then, all of a sudden, a whole new element showed up. . . . Some of them had, for example, the lids of garbage pails and sticks, and they were beating on them and were making an incredible noise." Birdseed scattered by protestors attracted gaggles of unwanted pigeons. One resident of the co-op said, "It was like the Hitchcock movie *The Birds*. The pigeons were bouncing off the windows."

After six days the co-op board grew tired of the scrutiny. Pale Male's fans' overwhelming outcry did the job. They had won. Following much negotiation and deliberation, it was decided that the nest would be replaced. "In hindsight, obviously, it was not a wise decision to remove the nest," admitted co-op board president Richard Cohen. The hawk watchers' world would soon be restored, and the nest's support was better than a mere patch job; instead, the co-op hired architect Dan Ionescu—at the cost of more than $40,000—to carefully construct a new platform on which the birds could build their home. "You don't get a call every day to design a nest," said Ionescu. Two weeks after the nest's removal, and after countless sketches and designs, Ionescu had created a new home for Pale Male and his family.

By the time the new platform was constructed, the story had been covered by numerous newspapers and was featured on multiple TV and radio shows. The small, pale hawk had done it. America was smitten. "It's a miracle on 74th Street," declared E. J. McAdams, the then executive director of New York City Audubon.

As time went by, things soon settled down. The birds and bird-watchers resumed their usual routines. But don't think Pale Male is forgotten. He is the star of an award-winning documentary and a bestselling book, and has been featured in countless articles by major newspapers around the world. He is a wild creature surviving in a man-made environment. "The idea that a feathered friend could find home amid stone and steel," wrote one journalist, "well, that's heartening, proof that even after eons of human depredation, warm-blooded creatures can still flourish alongside our cold technology." And perhaps it's even simpler. "It's a miracle" is a phrase overheard oftentimes at the Boat Pond. If you go to Central Park in the springtime and join the hawk watchers, perhaps you, too, will utter, "It's a miracle."